HOW TO PROFITABLE BLOG

A Guide To Create Content That Rocks, Build Traffic, And Turn Your Blogging Passion Into Profit

Contents

Introduction

I want to thank you and congratulate you for downloading the book, *"How to Start A Profitable Blog: A Guide To Create Content That Rocks, Build Traffic, And Turn Your Blogging Passion Into Profit.*

This book contains valuable information on how to create passive income with a blog. After reading this book, you should have the understandings of what a blog is, and how to create passive income online. Keep in mind, when creating your blog, to focus on creating value, instead of just trying to make money. Creating value is important, because in order for you to get what you want, you have to first give others what they want. And know, that when your passive income exceeds your expenses, that is when you'll be financially free to replace your day job for life.

The phrase financial freedom includes the word financial, but it also includes the word freedom: Freedom to explore the blessings that surround us. Freedom to help ourselves so that we can help others. Freedom to live the life we choose to lead, instead of having to live the life that was chosen for us.

Thanks again for downloading this book, I hope it inspires you to create, and to follow your dreams.

CHAPTER ONE: GETTING STARTED WITH BLOGGING

"Self expression has become the new entertainment"
– Arianna Huffington

Almost everybody is a blogger these days – irrespective of the fact whether they realize it or not.

Have you ever written something on Facebook and received a few likes and may be some comments as well?

Awesome! You are a blogger.

Did you ever tweet a short sentence on Twitter?

Congratulations! You are a micro blogger!

How about uploading a YouTube video where you can obtain a few subscribers and prompt a few comments?

Well – you have begun videoblogging too!

Blogging leads to an outburst of expression and creativity, which in turn opens up digital doors for an expert who has till now been invisible.

And the best part – you do not have to wait for twenty five long years in order to be declared as an expert in a particular field. *Just declare yourself and publish*.

Isn't it easy?

Let us first try and understand the whole concept – **what is a blog and why so much hype around blogging**?

A blog is short for Web log. In layman terms, it is just a website with entries listed in a reverse chronological order. The original idea behind the creation of a blog was to create an online diary or journal that could be updated every day.

During the past few years, a number of software companies have developed platforms that have made the process of blogging extremely simple – you write your story, click 'submit,' and voila – it shows on your blog for the world to take notice of you and your 0brand.

But I am not a techie?

No problem. You don't worry on that front since most bloggers do not understand any programming language and the companies that have developed these platforms acknowledge that.

Starting a blog can be one of the simplest processes to start a website. It is quick to set up and sometimes completely free.

Even if there are steps to follow, they are extremely simple and then, there are plenty of resources to help you along the way.

Here are some interesting facts about blogs:

- Every half a second – a new blog is created somewhere in the world.
- This signifies an addition of 172,800 blogs to the internet every day.
- As on date, there are 152 million blogs on the internet.

Still thinking about the process? Well, if there are so many blog, the process just cannot be difficult.

THE COSTS INVOLVED

A number of services are available in order to empower you to start your blog – and that too for free. If you are simply going to be experimenting with the entire process of blogging, I would recommend a free service in order to first understand the process.

Once you get your feet wet and decide to stick with it and eventually make money with your blog, you can upgrade yourself to a self-hosted blog.

Getting a self-hosted blog is inexpensive – the domain name costs around $10 per year and webhosting is approximately a few bucks every month.

THE BLOGGING PLATFORMS

Well, if you are looking at creating a great blog and generating some passive income from it too, then I would suggest that you do not waste time with Blogger.com or WordPress.com . You will eventually want to change it – the sooner you do, the better it is for your blog.

I personally recommend being self-hosted on WordPress.org - this is more or less the industry standard today. You would need to pay a few dollars a month for hosting, but the income that you will generate eventually makes up for the expenses. Try and pick up a .com name that matches your site name.

Once you set up your blog on WordPress, you begin the process of content creation. This is in fact the most critical part of your blog. Remember, people will come for killer content – they definitely may get impressed by the pretty design or layout, however, that is not something that will get them back – only killer content can get them back and even generate some referrals.

The next thing that you need is an amazing layout and design. I recommend that you hire someone to help you with this process (unless, of course you are a graphic designer yourself). An experienced designer can help you create a layout that becomes a visual representation of your content, your feelings, your personality, yourself!

WHAT SHOULD YOU WRITE ABOUT?

Well, the best thing to begin with is to create amazing, compelling content – content that brings your readers back to your blog. This implies that your blog has to be truly awesome. The key here is to discover what 'awesome' means to you. Everyone has a passion – something that they are too good at, something that they can share and that their readers can learn from.

Discover your true passion and decide on a topic. Remember, everything that you publish should be meaningful – there has to be a definite intention behind whatever you decide to publish. The content has to be amazing and should add value to the readers.

Here are some questions that you can ask yourself before deciding on the subject for your blog:

- What is it that you love to do most?
- What are the things that you are really passionate about?
- What are the topics that people ask you for advice?
- What are the subjects that you are naturally drawn towards?
- What subjects do you love to read most?
- What gets you so fired up that you can't stop talking about?

You must also have a clear plan on what you want to write about. This will include a main topic, then a few sub topics and then a few categories beneath each subtopic.

Let us take an example here – If your main topic is 'Living well on a budget,' your sub-topics could be 'Using coupons to your advantage,' 'DIY recipes', 'Tips to declutter your home,' 'Ideas to save money during the holiday season,' etc. Now, here the main theme is pretty broad and includes a couple of sub themes – however, it does not include everything.

Therefore, the readers of the blog are aware of what to expect when they visit the blog.

Now, imagine this blog owner starting with movie reviews and then reviews of latest makeup and gadgets and then reviews of various restaurants in the town. This will only confuse the reader and they will think that the blog owner does not understand their content too well.

Therefore, *it is important to have a clear structure and plan in place*.

Readers always crave authenticity – don't hold things back, be authentic and give everything that you have got. Just focus on making your blog awesome.

Go through the blogs that you love but never try and BE those blogs. *Be your own voice – be authentic – be passionate – focus on your individual strengths that can make your readers life awesome*.

So, let us review the action items from this chapter:

- Spend some time with yourself, trying to discover your passion which will translate into your blog's main theme, sub theme and sub topics.
- Pick up a great blog name and set up a self-hosted blog on WordPress.org
- If you are not a graphic designer, get professional help with the layout and design.
- Create compelling content that is truly awesome and adds value to your readers.

CHAPTER TWO: CREATING CONTENT THAT ROCKS

Alright, for a moment – let us think about your favorite blog. *Is there a blog that you are always dying to read – that you check out even before a new post is released?*

Now, take a moment to think about the things that you love in this blog.

- Does this blog have a cool theme?
- Do you love the font that they use?
- Is it their choice of colors?
- Do you like the fact that they have over five thousand Facebook followers?

Well, the blog may have all of that, but chances are that you are solely captivated by the content. You love to read stuff that you can relate to, don't you? You love to read stuff that adds value. You love to read through those mouth-watering recipes or DIY household projects and can't wait to try some yourself. You love commenting on the blog post and sharing your results. In fact, you have even accepted the thirty days de-clutter challenge and are fully motivated to share your results.

In simple language, your favorite blog rocks because it contains content that rocks!

Try and create content that can add value, that you are passionate about and that your readers can benefit from.

My next suggestion for you is to create a **calendar of events** for your blog.

But, I can only write when I am in a mood!

True, most bloggers start like that. They decide to write only if they are in a mood to write. Mostly, the result is an unorganized blog where readers do not know what to expect and when to expect.

My suggestion here is that if you are serious about blogging and looking to earn some money through your passion, you must create a calendar of events. It could be a simple word or excel document where you mention about what you would post every day.

Here is an example:

September 2015

Week one:

- Monday: Monday morning mantra – simple 30 minute yoga for the week
- Tuesday: Tuesday healthy tips – Healthy tips from the kitchen
- Wednesday: Wednesday Recipe – Healthy Wednesday recipe – banana oatmeal with kale and orange smoothie

- Thursday: Things no one will tell you about hormones and PMS (yes, it is impacting your relationships but not anymore!)
- Friday: Friday family fun: Fun exercises for the whole family
- Saturday: Tips to encourage your kids towards healthy eating (bonus: healthy blueberry pie recipe)
- Sunday: no post

You could even use different colored highlighters to ensure that posts that are in progress stand out and posts that have been completed and posted are hidden or highlighted in a different color. I like to use a green highlighter for posts that are in progress, a red highlighter for posts that are due but not started and a blue highlighter for posts that have been completed.

Ideally, your calendar must be planned at least two months in advance and posts should be written at least a fortnight in advance. It may be necessary to shuffle things up a little, however, make sure to stick to the plan as much as possible.

Adequate planning can ensure that you are sticking to the plan even when on a break. Imagine, how cool it would be to post something on your blog as you holiday with family on the mountains or at the beach. All you need to do is pick up a post that you have already written and plug it in there.

Now, you may think that it is going to be difficult to come up with two months of awesome, brand new content. Well, the key here is **effective brainstorming**. Every week, you must set aside some time for yourself. This is the time when you will be at your peak capacity. Keep loads of colored sticky notes on a table and write down your blog sub categories. Now, for the next half an hour, just think about what your readers would want to see from you in the next fifteen days or so. Write down whatever comes into your mind. If you cannot think about anything for a particular category, leave it blank and come back to it later.

Now, take all your sticky notes and get organized. Use the next half an hour to convert these ideas into catchy titles for your blogpost.

Remember, this method of brainstorming is not cast in stone. You may like to brainstorm as you clean the house or every day in the shower. That is totally your call. Decide on what works best for you and work accordingly.

TIPS TO WRITING A GREAT BLOG POST

Let me say this upfront – if you dislike writing, then probably blogging is not meant for you. In order to write a blog post, you need to practice the discipline of writing. Decide on a time every day and force yourself to write a certain number of words – I like to write around a 1,000 words at a time. This makes two blog posts a day – one in the morning and one in the evening. Depending on your goals, you could decide on your daily target and make sure that you meet it –

practicing to write a certain number of words every day will greatly elevate your writing style.

A fantastic blog post means greater traffic on your blog, more pins on Pinterest, more Facebook shares and more tweets. *The impact of all this?*

All these help your blog to grow.

Here are some of the things that you must do as you write a blog post:

Your post must make a clear point: Sometimes, writers keep writing about a number of things and towards the end, the reader gets lost – thinking – *"well, what was he really trying to say?"* To maintain the interest of your readers, write blog posts that make a point. These posts can be easily summarized in one sentence.

Your post must be visually appealing: You must ensure that your blog posts carry amazing images to go with them. With the advent of Pinterest, this is an important factor for all your posts.

Your posts must teach ONE simple lesson: Now, I am not trying to discourage you from writing about complicated projects and ideas. However, with time I have realized that you receive maximum traffic on posts that are really simple – just one simple lesson is all that people want to read through one post.

Your posts must evoke an emotional response: Most posts that generate traffic are the ones that make people feel a certain way – they could make you happy, sad, angry, empathetic, grateful or encouraged. Make sure that people are able to relate to what you write and your post generates an emotional response.

Your posts make your readers go WOW: It is better to share one blog post that generates a WOW response than post many that do not stir up any feelings or conversations. Write about things that you are passionate about and that your readers can't help but pay attention to – *they must be able to stop everything and just focus on your post.*

Your posts should encourage and empower your readers: Imagine sharing a really nice picture with a really complicated recipe. Since the picture is nice, it definitely attracts attention. But the recipe? Well, your readers lose interest the moment they begin reading it. It is too complicated to follow and they cannot relate to it. *They don't see themselves preparing that dish!*

How about including some tips that can make the recipe simple? You could even write about the difficulties that you faced and the steps that you took in in order to overcome those.

Your readers have to feel that they CAN do it too!

Your posts must be unique and interesting: Your posts must have something amazing, new and interesting to say. Ideally, after reading your post your readers must be able to look at a problem in a manner that they have never done before.

One of the most important things to remember is that you must create killer content each time you intend to create a post. Your content should be able to draw traffic to your blog – you must therefore write posts that get loads of comments, Facebook shares, pins and can get easily optimized for search engines.

In a nutshell, this would mean:

Amazing content = Killer blog post = Viral traffic = Great money

Reviewing some of the key action items from this chapter:

- Create a calendar of events and use it religiously
- Schedule a brainstorming session with yourself every week
- Write every single day – whether you like it or not, discipline is the key
- Create killer content that can get viral traffic

CHAPTER THREE: KEEPING IT CLEAN – PLAIN AND SIMPLE

Well, we live in a visual world and we like to see everything well organized. Here is the bitter truth – you can create an amazing calendar, write awesome content and maintain an incredible level of discipline. However, if the entire package does not sell….well, you are doomed.

Imagine a reader visiting your blog. Now, this is what they notice – there are five main colors, with some really pretty flowers in the background, colorful stripes in the header and a long footer that makes absolutely no sense. So, even though they are reading killer content, they are distracted by too much information available on your blog.

Your site may seem to be the most appealing site on earth to you, but it is definitely not pretty if your readers find it cluttered.

I would suggest a clean, simple, organized, easy to navigate design with fewer colors and more white space.

If you have been blogging for some time now, it is time to take a step back and reflect upon the following questions:

- Is your blog too cluttered or unorganized?
- Does your navigation make sense?

- Can your readers locate what they are looking for?
- Are your fonts easy to read?
- Can a newcomer visiting your blog get an idea (in thirty seconds) of what your blog is about and the kind of posts they can expect?
- Do all your posts have a clear call to action?
- Are your images high quality, appealing images?

The navigation toolbar in your blog should make things extremely easy for your readers. They must be able to find posts that they are looking for in just thirty seconds.

Take some time to create categories and then fit those categories into subtopics. Categorize every post and eliminate categories that do not make sense. Highlight your best content in a manner that it stands out. How about including a 'most popular posts' section on your sidebar?

Wrap your content in a tasteful manner – a manner that people want to see. This means that your content must be presented in a neat and organized manner.

Here are some great and neat blog designs that I love:

http://moneysavingmom.com/

http://www.ahaparenting.com/blog

http://andthenwesaved.com/

As you notice the above designs, you will see that none of these blogs look alike. _The only common thing in these blogs is that they let their content show through_.

As you get to creating and maintaining your blog, you must understand the importance of images that you will use on your blog.

Here are some photography rules that you must stick to:

Invest in a good camera: Investing in a great camera is extremely important – your camera must be able to provide high quality images that your readers will drool over.

Be aware of the lightening: Good lightening is immensely important as you get ready to click a picture. Try and get most of your shoots in bright, indirect light.

Get a clean background: As you get ready to click a picture, make sure that the background is not distracting. A clean, organized background is important for a great image.

Try and make your images Pin-worthy. Remember, when used correctly, Pinterest is more powerful than Facebook, Google+ or Twitter.

Pin-worthy posts are always a combination of great content and captivating images.

Colorful images capture more attention than monochromatic ones. Warm colors are more likely to be re-pinned than cool colors. Close up shots and pins without faces stand a greater chance to be re-pinned.

Now, here is the thing – people collect and pin images they like – only because these images look super appealing to them. Converting your pins to page views implies that you have gone a step ahead and used Pinterest to the fullest.

Here are some examples of great images – the ones that are generally re-pinned and generate more traffic:

Source: www.pinterest.com

Oooh we love the glittery tights! Add these to any outfit to take you from office to the Christmas Party! #Christmas #party

Peanut Butter Fudge cake- I Love the combination of chocolate and peanut butter!

And now, time for visiting the action items from this chapter:

- You must revisit your blog design and develop a plan on the changes that you would like.
- Ensure that your design is simple and clean – free from unnecessary clutter.
- Create a well thought out navigation bar that tells your readers where to find stuff that they are looking for.
- Create pin-worthy blog posts - using content that rocks and high quality images that attract attention.

CHAPTER FOUR: BUILDING TRAFFIC

Before I begin talking about the limitless ways to build traffic to your blog, it is important to mention that you must not try to grow your platform if your blog is not ready yet.

Always remember that sustainable blog traffic growth can only happen if your content rocks. Having somebody visit your blog once is just one thing – but having them to come back again and again is another and that is the reason why awesome content is a necessity if you want to profit from your blog.

Here are some of the traditional ways to build traffic on your blog:

WORD OF MOUTH

Word of mouth is a great way to start building traffic on your blog – you tell your friends about your blog, who in turn tell their family and friends and that is how your list of readers increases – in case your content is read worthy.

Before you begin talking to people about your blog, spend some time crafting your elevator pitch. This is a thirty second overview of what your blog is about and how readers can benefit from it. Once you are ready with the pitch, practice it, hone it and own it.

Here are some ideas about how to build word of mouth publicity for your blog:

- How about sending a quick reminder to everyone in your address book whenever you publish a new blog post?
- Every time, you publish a new blog post, share it with a comment on your Facebook page and ask for feedback from relatives and friends.
- Have an inexpensive bumper sticker printed with your web address – this is how a number of people with get to know about your blog and begin reading it.
- Politely ask people you know and trust to spread the word around – you could ask them in person or include a link at the end of each blog post.

Remember, most first time bloggers feel embarrassed promoting their blog and asking for feedback. This is completely natural and should not discourage you from seeking support. Your friends may even mock at you initially. Once again, don't get discouraged by this and just continue promoting your blog. Think of it as your business and promote it as if you were promoting any other business.

COMMENTING ON OTHER BLOGS

You may have heard about shameless commenting on other, bigger blogs in order to drive traffic.

Well, here is the deal – while bloggers pretty much love to get comments, it is important to realize that they hate spammers – you just CANNOT scam the traffic these seasoned bloggers worked incredibly hard to build.

A better approach here is to read the blogs that you like – especially the ones that you feel have a great crossover traffic – and leave a thoughtful comment with your blog URL only if you genuinely have to say something. This means that your comments have to be genuine, straight from your heart. If your comments are genuine and insightful, they may lead other readers from the blog to reach out to you via your blog.

PROMOTE OTHER BLOGS

If you already have a sound database of readers, this 'pay it forward' approach can work wonders for your own blog.

Promoting another blogger can be as simple as linking back to another blogger whose post inspired any of your posts. Most blogs have trackbacks on their blog posts – this means that if you link a person's blog, they will automatically get a notification that you linked their blog. Now, I can't vouch for others, but whenever I receive such an alert, I definitely go and check the blog of the person who linked me. And that is human psychology – *most people do that, by default!*

Remember, the more you focus on building other people's blogs without accepting anything in return – the more it comes back to you in many different ways.

NETWORKING

Networking can open new doors for your blogging business. Apart from forging genuine friendships, you get the opportunity to grow your blog. I must mention here that 'true, genuine friendships' come first. If you make friends with the intention of growing your business, your friends can see right through your eyes.

The best way to connect with other bloggers is via blog conferences. This is a highly misunderstood profession and I can't tell you how amazing it is to be in the company of like-minded people who understand what you do for a living.

Here are few things that you can do at your first networking event:

Focus on making new connections: Even though you will be tempted to attend all sessions in order to make up for the money that you spent, don't fall into the trap and if possible, spend some time going out for coffee with the girl you met at breakfast or taking a small nap because you were busy chatting all night with your roommate, who is now your friend.

Find a roommate: Most blogging conferences have Facebook groups with a roommate connection thread – use that and get a roommate. Even if you and your roommate do not convert into overnight best friends, there is something really comforting about knowing at least one person in the group.

Listen more, speak less: The best way to learn is through listening – ask as many questions as you can and listen to the answers in the most genuine manner possible. There is a reason God gave us two ears and one mouth.

Listening and being genuinely interested in the conversation is a gift that you can give to other people at the conference and in the process, this can help you win genuine friends too. You will also be amazed at the amount of learning this can get you.

Engage in meaningful conversations: Imagine meeting a new person and just handing over your business card. What a turn off!

Focus on real conversations, not card swapping. I don't even keep the cards of people who I have not had a great conversation with. If you are genuinely interested in developing a relationship and don't know what to say, ask a question.

Don't let your new found friendship fade away: If you get a chance to develop authentic connections and are lucky enough to find somebody as amazing as you are, don't let the friendship fade away after the conference. Start reading their blogs, read their comments, send an occasional 'Hi', connect on Facebook – nurture the relationship.

GUEST POSTS

If done properly, guest posts have an amazing potential to drive traffic to your own blog. The key to a great guest post is to not post on a site with a similar audience but to write something so great that your host's readers are driven to your site in order to read more of what you write. If you are interested in guest posting on other sites, make sure that you ask for guidelines and always submit original content. Also, do not try to be overly familiar – since this is not 'your' audience. You are writing for somebody else's audience. Submit your best content and never make your post self-promotional.

BUILD YOUR E MAIL LIST

'Building an email list' model is extremely impactful when you want to reach out to an audience that can be converted into a sales funnel that you want to use in order to sell your expensive courses or physical products. This model is extremely effective for online marketers. However, for stay at home mommy's, this model may sometimes backfire – most of them will NEVER be interested in buying a $450 course.

Having said that, I still feel that building an email list is important. You can connect with your audience via newsletters and share news about your upcoming e-books and courses. I personally use Aweber to build my list, but I have also heard raving reviews about MailChimp.

As you build your email list, remember to place the subscribe button at a prominent place in your blog. Create some nice freebies for your subscribers – these could range from recipe books to goal setting and time management guides – just make sure that you are adding value to your readers.

Always promote the incentive that you offer on social media

UNDERSTAND SEARCH ENGINE OPTIMIZATION

As you create content, remember to create content that is SEO friendly. You must remember that Google's only goal is to display the best possible content for a particular search. The extremely sophisticated Google algorithms look at everything ranging from the content on the web page to the time visitors spent on the page. Another important thing to remember is that Google cannot be tricked via SEO. Here are some things that you must know in order to create a blog post that is Search Engine Optimized.

Title Tag: The title tag refers to words that show up at the very top of your browser window when you open a particular web page. The default title tag is generally the title of your post. However, it can be further optimized – remember that you can change the title tag and make it as long as you want, but Google will only read the first seventy characters. *You must* *therefore focus on optimizing the first seventy characters.*

Meta description: The default meta description is the first 150 words of your post. You can change it too – it helps in telling Google what your post is about.

Meta Keywords: Meta keywords are the search phrases that you like to see associated with your post. They are more helpful in browsers such as Yahoo or Bing.

UNDERSTANDING THE POWER OF SOCIAL MEDIA

You may probably be familiar with the numerous options of social media – Facebook, Twitter, Pinterest, Instagram, Google+, StumbleUpon, LinkedIn, Snapchat, Reddit, etc.

Now, here is the point – I do not want you to use all the options listed here. In fact, most social media is a waste of time. Since you are treating your blog as your business, your time on social media must be measured in terms of ROI. You may have over a million Twitter followers. However, if none of them translate into readers….well, no point then!

You must work on developing your presence on platforms where your readers tend to be. As an example, for blogs targeted at women aged between 25-55, the ideal social media platform would be Facebook or Pinterest. For a blog that focuses on entrepreneurs or job seekers between the age group

25-40, the ideal social media platform would be LinkedIn.

Figure out where your audience is and use that platform – you want them to come back to your blog and read about what you have to offer.

As you focus on building your followers, remember *it is always quality that matters over quantity*. While it seems nice to have over one million followers (and I am sure a lot of them would be disengaged), it is nicer to have around 10,000 actively engaged followers.

As you build your Pinterest home page or your Facebook page, make sure that you use your blog name as your Pinterest and Facebook name. Be sure to include your blog address too.

Join as many collaborative boards as you can and be active – pin the relevant content on multiple boards. You could join the Pinterest Collaborative Boards group on Facebook.

And now, time for action plan from this chapter:

- Start talking about your blog with family and friends. Have some business cards printed and create an elevator pitch. Practice it at least once every day and OWN it.
- Read and comment on other people's blogs.
- Promote other bloggers by featuring their posts, or linking to a blog post that you really liked.
- Attend blog conferences, network with other bloggers and make friends.

- Create an incentive for people who subscribe to your e mail list (this could be anything from a free book or course to a physical item that they avail when they purchase something)
- Optimize your website and each blog post that you write, being careful not to spam your readers with a bunch of keywords.
- Do not focus on each and every social media platform available out there. Instead, focus on the platforms that can get you maximum readers.
- Determine your objectives before going for a paid Facebook promotion.
- Work on converting your new visitors into regular blog readers.

CHAPTER FIVE: HONEY, WHERE IS THE MONEY?

If you have managed to build a great blog with some awesome traffic, then the possibilities to monetize your blog can be limitless.

If you are really looking at building your blog for profit, then it is important to understand that rushing things up might not help. Almost all full time bloggers (who use their blog to earn a living), have been regularly blogging for at least three years now. It takes time to build steady traffic that can help you earn a living. You may choose to run advertisements, use affiliate links or work with brands from day one, but you must remember that the traffic that you get on your blog will ultimately determine your ability to monetize your blog.

Therefore, the first thing that you must concentrate on is to 'Go Slow.' Stay away from the quick fix money making hacks and focus on the big picture. Look at how you can create awesome content and ensure that you are building your base of readers. Do not agree to write sponsored posts or host giveaways for products that you are not even convinced about but can get you some quick bucks. Instead, focus on writing content that gets more readers.

Substantial research has been conducted to prove that there is a definite relationship between the number of monthly page views a blog gets and the amount of money the blog owner earns.

Let us look at some of the methods that can help you in monetizing your blog (once you have enough readers):

Ad Networks: Advertising networks such as Google AdSense, Media.net , PulsePoint.com , BlogHer, etc. work with a large number of advertisers who pay the network to place their ad on your site. Depending on the ad network, you could receive a cost per thousand views or a pay per click payment. Sometimes, it is a combination of these two things.

Once your advertisements are in place, you do not have to do anything. You make money by simply sitting there. The only flipside to this is the inconsistent ad traffic. If you happen to be at the right place at the right time, you may earn a lot of money for a while. However, as trends begin to fall, your income may begin to fluctuate.

This implies that revenue from ad networks is incredible when you can capture it. It also implies that you need to exercise caution as you rely on revenue from advertisements. You must diversify your income.

Therefore, if you want to earn profit from your blog, you can let the ad network be your important revenue stream, but you can never let it be your only revenue stream.

The highest paying ad network is Google AdSense.

BlogAds allows bloggers to sell their ad space, set their own prices, and even reject or accept ads.

As you begin using these ad networks, you must learn to optimize the placement of these advertisements – so that you get maximum clicks and revenue. Research proves that the best placement is directly above, below, or to the left of your primary blog content. Make sure to use a darker color for ad placements.

You can also use content based advertising. Remember, users who visit your blog for its content are more likely to click on the relevant products that you advertise on your blog.

Private advertising: Private advertising is any paid advertisement or link on your site that is paid directly by the company that is advertising, rather than a network. It is generally a specific ad at a specific spot that stays up for a limited period of time.

In order to work with brands directly, you must clearly define your brand strategy and figure out nice, innovative ways through which you could offer private advertising on your website in the most authentic manner possible.

You must be able to determine how you want to work with brands. In order to sell your site to various brands, spend some time packaging your blog. Create an attractive advertising booklet that provides the brands you intend to work with, with a description of your blog along with the traffic statistics and opportunities available. You may want to consider setting up a specific email address solely for the purpose of advertising requests.

Affiliate advertising: Affiliate advertising is an ad or a link to a product or a company that results in a commission only if the click on that ad leads to a sale. This could include Amazon links or links through other websites such as Pepperjam Network , ShareASale, E Junkie, etc.

The most successful affiliate sales are a result of creating a relationship of trust with your readers. Your readers will buy the things that you recommend because they trust you – they trust what you write and are happy with the manner in which you keep them engaged.

The payout for Amazon sales is fairly low (around 5%) in comparison to other affiliate programs. However, the best thing about Amazon is their user friendly interface which allows you to link to link to any of their pages or products. Now, imagine somebody clicking on the affiliate link, reaching the Amazon site, and in the process of surfing for a $5 book, buying a $500 coffee machine!

Yes…this is also possible with Amazon – they sell everything under the sun and the person who bought the coffee machine used your affiliate link, which means you get a commission on that. *Cool, isn't it?*

The only way to increase your affiliate sales is by producing awesome content and paying attention to the kind of things that your readers are using and buying. Be honest with your readers and share links for things that you actually use or places that you actually visit. Always ensure that your links are relevant.

Sponsored posts and Brand promotion: Another popular monetization strategy is to work directly with brands to promote their products within a post or series of posts. These can be posts that are written on a topic provided by the sponsor, product reviews, or paid product giveaways.

Selling products: You could use your blog to sell your e-books, your e-courses or even items such as t-shirts, tote bags, handmade decorative items, etc. And the results are self-explanatory – you get to market your products via your blog, and you also get to earn awesome profits – with practically zero investment.

Selling services: Depending on the niche that you are comfortable with, you could sell services such as local classes, hobby ideas or even online consulting services such as virtual feng shui and vaastu consultation.

Writing and Speaking opportunities: Many popular speakers get their first speaking assignment through writing a successful blog post. You never know, you may be the next one in the line!

Let us look at some of the action items from this chapter:

- You must take it slow – realize the every blogger earns income differently and almost nobody earns it overnight.
- Figure out what resources you would like to use and decide accordingly. You do not have to use all monetization channels. Identify the voice of your blog and see what fits best.
- Be authentic with your readers – do not advertise products that you do not believe in or would not use personally.

CHAPTER SIX: STAYING ORGANIZED AND AIMING FOR THE PERFECT WORK LIFE INTEGRATION

Well, blogging seems to be an incredibly easy profession. You can be sitting in your PJs, sipping your cup of coffee, watching over your adorable kids and still be working.

The best piece of advice that I have ever received when it comes to blogging is to work smarter. There are only 24 hours in a day and when you are blogging for profit, there is always so much that can still be done.

We live in an extremely connected world, so the process of liking a friend's blog, or commenting on somebody's blog or even responding to a comment that you just received on your blog, can become a 24/7 activity.

Think about your blog as your business and set your own boundaries. Create work timings and be strict with yourself.

Create a to-do list and ensure that you follow your daily calendar or events.

Do not procrastinate and get the big things accomplished first.

Take regular breaks and delete what is not essential (or not important) in the important/ urgent matrix.

Aim at bringing your inbox to zero every single day.

And most important, *give yourself permission to enjoy life – to get out of your home office and have some fun. You do not have to get everything done. And you must be prepared for that.*

Before You Go...

Thank you again for downloading this book!

I hope this book was able to help give you an understanding of how to blog for profit and replace your day job for life.

Finally, if you enjoyed this book, then I'd like to ask you for a favor, would you be kind enough to leave a review for this book on Amazon? It'd be greatly appreciated!

http://www.amazon.com/review/create-review?ie=UTF&&asin=B00ZVE2G8E

Thank you and good luck!

Check Out My Other Books

Below you'll find one of my other #1 Amazon bestseller books that is popular on Amazon and Kindle as well.

How To Raise Your Credit Score: The Ultimate Guide To Your Total Money Makeover. End Your Money Problems- Be Debt Free Forever! Get This Book for a low price of ONLY, $1.99. Read on your PC, Mac, Smartphone, Tablet, or Kindle Device- Download Your Copy Today!

http://www.amazon.com/gp/product/B00Y6YS5YO/

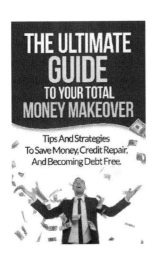

Made in the USA
Monee, IL
17 September 2021